The Manson Famil

"Then and Now"

Written By

David Pietras
All Rights Reserved
© 2013

*"I'm probably one of the most dangerous men in the world if I want to be.
But I never wanted to be anything but me."*

Charles Manson

Murder of a movie star

Quiet and secluded is just what the young movie star wanted. The canyons above Beverly Hills were far enough away from the noisy glitz of Hollywood to afford some privacy and space. Sharon Tate loved this place on Cielo Drive. To her it meant romance — romance with the man of her dreams and the father of her child, director Roman Polanski.

Charles Manson

It was cooler up there too, which was especially refreshing on that hot muggy Saturday night, the 9th of August 1969. The beautiful young woman kept herself company with her attractive and sophisticated friends: Abigail Folger, the coffee heiress and her boyfriend Voytek Frykowski, and an internationally known hair stylist Jay Sebring.

Sharon was eight months pregnant and very lonely for her husband who was away in Europe working on a film. Impromptu gatherings like this one on a weekend night were not at all unusual.

The house was deliberately secluded but not completely insecure. Approximately 100 feet from the house was a locked gate and on the property was a guesthouse inhabited by an able-bodied young caretaker.

That night the Kotts, Sharon's nearest neighbors who lived about 100 yards away, thought they heard a few gunshots coming from the direction of Sharon's property sometime between 12:30 and 1 A.M. But since they heard nothing else, they went to bed.

Around the same time, a man supervising a camp-out less than a mile away heard a chilling scream: "Oh, God, no, please don't! Oh, God, no, don't, don't..."

He drove around the area, but found nothing unusual.

Nearby a neighbor's dogs went into a barking frenzy somewhere between 2 and 3 A.M. He got out of bed and looked around, but found nothing amiss and went back to bed.

A private security guard hired by some of the wealthy property owners thought he heard several gunshots a little after 4 A.M. and called his headquarters. Headquarters, in turn, called Los Angeles Police Department to report the disturbance. The LAPD officer said: "I hope we don't have a murder; we just had a woman-screaming call in that area."

The Tate/Polanski House on Cielo Drive

Winifred Chapman, Sharon Tate's housekeeper, got to the main gate of the house a little after 8 A.M. She noticed what looked like a fallen telephone wire hanging over the gate. She pushed the gate control mechanism and it swung open. As she walked up to the house, she saw an unfamiliar white Rambler parked in the driveway.

When she got to the house, she took the house key from its hiding place and unlocked the back door. Once inside the kitchen, she picked up the telephone and confirmed that it was a telephone wire that had fallen, completely knocking out all phone service. As she made her way toward the living room, she noticed that the front door was open and that there were splashes of red everywhere. Looking out the front door, she saw a couple of pools of blood and what appeared to be a body on the lawn.

She shrieked and ran back through the house and down the driveway, passing close enough to the Rambler to see that there was yet another body inside the car. She ran over to the Kotts and banged on the door, but they were not home, so she ran to the next house and did the same thing, screaming hysterically.

The Crime Scene

10050 Cielo Drive

Victims: Sharon Tate, Jay Sebring, Abigail Folger, Voytek Frykowski and Steve Parent

LAPD Officer Jerry DeRosa arrived first. He walked up to the Rambler and found a young man slumped toward the passenger side, drenched in blood.

Steve Parent

At this point, Officer William Whisenhunt joined DeRosa. The two officers, with guns drawn searched the other automobiles and the garage, while a third officer Robert Burbridge caught up with them.

There on the beautifully manicured lawn with its magnificent panorama of Los Angeles lay two bodies. One was a white man that appeared to be in his thirties. Someone had battered in his head and face, while savagely puncturing the rest of his body with dozens of wounds.

Voytek Frykowski

The other body was that of a young woman with long brown hair lying in a full-length nightgown with multiple stab wounds.

Abigail Folger

The three officers cautiously approached the house. No telling what or who may be waiting in there for them. It would have been foolhardy for all of them to enter through the front door. However, as they went near the front door, they saw that one of the front window screens had been removed. Whisenhunt found an open window on the side of the house where he and Burbridge made their entry.

Once the other two officers were inside, DeRosa approached the front door. On the lower half of the door, he saw scrawled in blood the word "PIG."

 In the hallway they found two large steamer trunks, a pair of horned rimmed glasses and pieces of a broken gun grip.

Then when they reached the couch, they were in for a real shock. A young blond woman, very pregnant, was laying on the floor, smeared all over with blood, a rope around her neck that extended over a rafter in the ceiling. The other end of the rope was around the neck of a man lying nearby, also drenched in blood.

Sharon Tate and Jay Sebring

As they looked through the rest of the house they heard a man's voice and the sound of a dog. It was William Garretson the caretaker. The officers handcuffed him and put him under arrest.

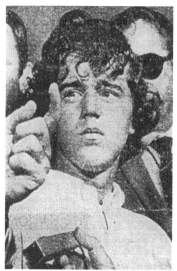

William Garretson

The photo with Roman Polanski as it appeared in Life magazine in 1969

The bodies of the victims being removed from the house

3301 Waverly Drive

Victims: Leno and Rosemary LaBianca

Later that Saturday night, Leno and Rosemary LaBianca and Susan Struthers, Rosemary's 21-year-old daughter, drove back from vacation trailering their boat.   They dropped off Susan at her apartment and drove home to 3301 Waverly Drive in the Los Feliz area of L.A.   They stopped to pick up a newspaper between 1 and 2 A.M.

3301 Waverly Drive

It wasn't until the next day that anybody came to the house to see them.   Frank Struthers, Rosemary's son by a previous marriage, got a ride home.   Around 8:30 P.M., as he carried his camping equipment up the driveway, he noticed things that worried him.   First the speedboat was still in the driveway.   It was very unlike his stepfather not to put the boat in the garage. Then Frank noticed that all the window shades were down — something his parents never did.

He knocked on the door, but got no answer, so he went to a pay phone and called, but again with no response. He finally got in touch with his sister, who came with her boyfriend to their parents' house.

Frank and the boyfriend found the back door open. They left Susan in the kitchen until they had a chance to look around. When the two young men walked into the living room, they saw Leno in his pajamas, lying with a pillow over his head and a cord around his neck. Something was sticking out from his stomach.

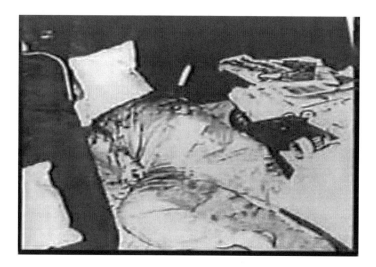

They rushed out of the house, dragging Susan with them and called the police at the neighbors' house.

Soon an ambulance and police cars arrived. Leno was found with a blood-drenched pillowcase over his head and the cord of a large lamp tied tightly around his neck. His hands had been tied behind him with a leather thong. A carving fork protruded from his stomach and the word "WAR" had been carved in his flesh.

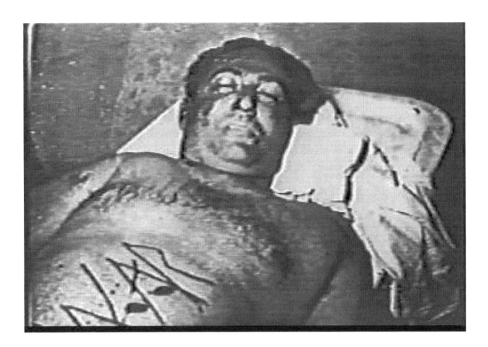

In the master bedroom, they found his wife Rosemary lying on the floor, her nightgown up over her head. She too had a pillowcase over her head and a lamp cord tied tightly around her neck.

In three places in the house, there was writing which appeared to be in the victims' blood: on the living room wall, "DEATH TO PIGS;" on another wall in the living room, the single word "RISE;" and in the refrigerator door, "HEALTHER SKELTER," misspelled.

The Slaughtered - Sharon Tate

Eventually, all of the victims of the massacre at Sharon Tate's home were identified. The young man in the car was a teenager named Steve Parent who had come to visit Garretson, the caretaker. The two victims found outside the house were Abigail Folger and her lover, Voytek Frykowski. In the living room joined by rope were Sharon Tate and Jay Sebring.

A .22 caliber gun had shot Steve Parent, Jay Sebring and Voytek Frykowski. Of the five victims, all but Steve Parent had been stabbed repeatedly. Sebring had been hit in the face and Frykowski had been repeatedly hit on the head with a blunt object.

The stab wounds suggested that only one knife had been used for the wounds. The nature of the wounds indicated that something like a bayonet was the weapon. A strange knife, a Buck brand clasp-type pocketknife that the housekeeper could not identify was found very close to Sharon Tate's body.

Sharon Tate

Sharon Tate had been a beauty all of her life. Even as a child she had won beauty contests. But her ambition was not to be a model but a movie actress. Finally in 1963 at the age of 22 she found a sponsor in Producer Martin Ransohoff. With Ransohoff's help, she landed parts in the series *Beverly Hillbillies* and *Petticoat Junction,* and the movies *The Americanization of Emily* and *The Sandpiper.*

In 1965, she got her chance at her first feature role in the Eye of the Devil with David Niven and Deborah Kerr. In this movie she played the part of a country girl with special magical powers. While in London in the summer of 1966 for the filming of the movie, she met Roman Polanski, who had just made his mark as a director of the movie Repulsion with Catherine Deneuve and Cul de Sac, which had won many European film awards.

Polanski put Sharon as the lead in his campy film The Fearless Vampire Killers. During this period she became Polanski's lover. This relationship lasted quite a long time and shortly after the filming of Rosemary's Baby, he and Sharon married. In 1969, they rented the house on Cielo Drive from Terry Melcher, Doris Day's son and moved in mid-February.

Sharon's career never skyrocketed the way Polanski's did even with her role as Jennifer in Valley of the Dolls. A good part of the reason her career was going nowhere is that she never had an opportunity to show off whatever acting skills she had. All the roles she had were ones in which all she had to do was look pretty. Her career took a backseat when she became pregnant. The baby and her husband became the center of her life.

She was a unique lady according to most everyone who knew her. In spite of her beauty and remarkable figure, she was a very down-to-earth woman with none of the phoniness normally associated with starlets. She was very sweet and a bit on the naïve side. Everyone seemed to like Sharon even in a jealous, bitchy town like Hollywood.

Sharon's life was ended by five stab wounds in her chest and back, which penetrated her heart, lungs and liver and caused massive internal hemorrhaging. The remaining eleven wounds simply added insult to her savaged body.

Her little boy, Paul Richard Polanski, died with her.

Abigail & Her Lover

Abigail Folger, Sharon's friend was twenty-five years old when she died. As heiress to the Folger coffee fortune, she had led a very comfortable life. She made her debut in San Francisco in 1961. She graduated from Radcliffe. Like many wealthy girls, she looked for something meaningful to do with her time and became very involved in social work.

Folger and Frykowski

In 1968, she met her lover Voytek Frykowski who introduced her to Sharon and Roman Polanski. She became an investor in Jay Sebring's men's toiletries and hair styling business.

Her social work in the ghettos of Los Angeles was beginning to get to her.

She started to feel that her contribution was futile in combatting the enormous problems of ignorance and poverty. She told her friends that she couldn't get away from her work at the end of the day. "The suffering gets under your skin," she said.

Her relationship with Frykowski was also a source of concern to her. The two of them had become much too dependent upon drugs. Both the frustrations of her social work and her problems with Voytek were the subject of her almost daily conversations with a psychiatrist. She had just about built up enough strength to break off her love affair and try to get her life back on track when twenty-eight stab wounds intervened.

Voytek Frykowski was thirty-two when he died. He had been a long-time friend of Roman's from Poland. He was, according to Polanski, "a man of little talent but immense charm." Always a playboy, he had no visible means of support, essentially living off Abigail's money. While he told people he was a writer, there was no evidence that he was anything but a very charming, extroverted and entertaining "druggie."

However dissipated his life was or charming his personality, it came to an abrupt end with two gunshot wounds, thirteen blows to the head and fifty-one stab wounds.

Jay Sebring

Jay Sebring

Jay Sebring was quite the opposite career-wise from Frykowski. He was the top men's hairstylist in the U.S. and was a major force in the development of a market for men's hair products and toiletries. His customers included Frank Sinatra, Peter Lawford, George Peppard, Paul Newman and Steve McQueen. His new company, Sebring International would franchise men's hair styling shops and his line of hair products.

He was known as a ladies man and dated many different women. One of those women had at one time been Sharon Tate, who broke off her relationship with Sebring when she became involved with Polanski.

There was another, darker side to Sebring's exuberant sex life. He would tie up his girlfriends and occasionally whip them before they had sex. In spite of his flashy, successful outward life, there was reason to suspect that the real Jay Sebring was lonely and insecure.

A gunshot wound and seven stab wounds liberated him from his insecurities.

More Victims

Steven Parent

Aside from Sharon Tate's baby, the youngest victim was 18-year-old Steven Earl Parent who lived with his father, mother and siblings in El Monte. At around 11:45 P.M. Saturday night, Parent had come onto the estate to visit William Garretson, the caretaker who was living in the guesthouse. Parent's hobby was hi-fi equipment and he wanted to show Garretson a radio he brought with him. Garretson wasn't interested and Parent left the guesthouse around 12:15 A.M.

The young man had just graduated from high school in June and worked several jobs so that he could go to college in the fall.

Instead he got four bullets from a .22 caliber revolver.

Leno LaBianca

Leno LaBianca was a respectable businessman. His father was the founder of State Wholesale Grocery Company and Leno went into the family business right out of college. He was a man who was well liked and did not appear to have any enemies. People described him as a quiet, conservative person.

He died from the multiple stab wounds, twenty-six in all.

Rosemary LaBianca

Rosemary LaBianca was an attractive 38-year-old woman of Mexican origin. She had been orphaned as a child and later adopted when she was twelve. She had worked as a carhop and a waitress. She met her first husband in the 1940's and had two children. After they were divorced in 1958, she met Leno when she was a waitress at the Los Feliz Inn.

Rosemary had become a very successful businesswoman. Not only did she run the profitable Boutique Carriage, but also her prudent investments in securities and commodities left her with an estate of $2.6 million. Not bad for someone who started life with no advantages and spent most of her career as a waitress and carhop.

She had been stabbed forty-one times, six of which were enough to have caused her death.

On two consecutive nights, seven innocent adults and one unborn child lost their lives in what seemed to be a senseless, motiveless crime.

However one feels about the lifestyles of the wealthy and glamorous, it is hard to imagine any social good coming from these vicious murders. Yet over the years, the perpetrators of these crimes and their persistent followers have tried to suggest that these killings were necessary and desirable.

This author hopes that nobody finishing this story will agree.

Suspicion

In his very thorough book on the case, *Helter Skelter*, Prosecutor Vincent Bugliosi heaps a great deal of fault upon the homicide detectives of the Los Angeles Police Department. One of the examples he provides is the LAPD's slowness to connect the Tate murders with the LaBianca murders the following night and with the murder of Gary Hinman a few days earlier. Some of this fault on the part of the LAPD apparently stemmed from its lack of cooperation with the Los Angeles County Sheriff's Office.

Victim Gary Hinman

The LAPD was approached shortly after the Tate-LaBianca murders by two LA Sheriff's Office detectives who told them of the July 31 murder of music teacher Gary Hinman. On the wall of the dead man's living room was written in his own blood "POLITICAL PIGGY," which seemed very similar to the words written at both the Tate and the LaBianca crimes scenes. Also, Hinman had been stabbed to death as had victims at the Tate and LaBianca homes.

Amazingly enough, the LAPD detectives refused to examine any connection between the deaths of Hinman and the people at the Tate house. Furthermore, the LaBianca murders were squarely in the territory of the LA Sheriff's Office and the LAPD had no interest.

Bobby Beausoleil

Had the LAPD detectives bothered to listen to the LA Sheriff's Office detectives, they would have heard that the Sheriff's Office had arrested a Bobby Beausoleil for the Hinman murder. A Beausoleil who had been living with a bunch of hippies led by Charles Manson. But, the LAPD had already decided that the Tate murders were a result of a drug deal gone bad and didn't want to hear about any hippies.

On the other hand, the LAPD had in custody one William Garretson, the caretaker on the Tate estate who claimed that he slept through the entire bloody ordeal. The case against the frightened young man never materialized after he passed a polygraph test.

Officials essentially discounted robbery as a motive for the crimes, even though Rosemary LaBianca's wallet and wristwatch were missing. In the two homes of these affluent victims there were many items of value, which had not been touched by the killers. Small amounts of cash lying around the Tate home were still in evidence and the purses and wallets of the Tate victims were intact.

The LAPD did investigate three alleged dope dealers that had once crashed a party at the Polanski's, but one by one the men were cleared of any involvement.

Likewise, Roman Polanski was interviewed for hours by the police and agreed to a polygraph examination. On August 15, he returned for the first time since the murders to the house on Cielo Drive, accompanied by psychic Peter Hurkos.

Polanski had been devastated by the loss of his wife and son and was enraged at the media circus that he walked into when he got back to the States. He lashed out at the newspapers for suggesting that he and his wife were Satanists, indulging in sex and drug orgies. "Sharon," he said, "was so sweet and so lovely that I didn't believe that people like that existed...She was beautiful without phoniness. She was fantastic. She loved me and the last few years I spent with her were the only time of true happiness in my life..."

He worried to the police that perhaps he was the target not Sharon. "It could be some kind of jealousy or plot or something. It couldn't be Sharon directly." Polanski did not believe that drugs were a motive for the crimes. His wife, although she had experimented with LSD before they met, was not a big drug user. "I can tell you without question," he told the police. "She took no drugs at all, except for pot, and not too much of that. And during her pregnancy there was no question, she was so in love with her pregnancy she would do nothing. I'd pour a glass of wine and she wouldn't touch it."

The Reward

One month after the murders, Polanski, along with other contributors such as Peter Sellers, Yul Brynner and Warren Beatty, put an ad in the LA area newspapers for a reward:

REWARD

$25,000

Roman Polanski and friends of the Polanski family offer to pay a $25,000 reward to the person or persons who furnish information leading to the arrest and conviction of the murderer or murderers of Sharon Tate, her unborn child, and the other four victims.

It seemed like it was open season on theories. Everybody had a theory. The Mafia did it, the Polish secret police, etc. Sharon's father, Colonel Paul Tate, a former Army intelligence officer, launched his own private investigation. Letting his hair grow long and growing a beard, he started to frequent the hippie joints, the drug markets, hoping that he would get some tidbit of information that would lead to the murderers of his beloved daughter and grandson.

On September 1, 1969, a 10-year-old boy found a gun on his lawn in Sherman Oaks. He carefully took the .22 caliber Hi Standard Longhorn revolver to his father, who immediately called the LAPD. The gun was dirty and rusty and had a broken gun grip.

A couple of weeks earlier, the LAPD forensics experts determined that the .22 caliber revolver with the broken grip used on the Tate victims was none other than a Hi Standard .22 caliber Longhorn revolver, which was relatively unique and rare. Amazingly enough, two weeks later, an identical gun with a broken grip is turned in to the LAPD, tagged, filed away and completely forgotten.

.22 caliber Longhorn revolver

A couple of days later, the LAPD sent out flyers to all personnel describing the murder gun and attaching a photo of the revolver. The flyer was also sent out to other law enforcement agencies around the country and Canada, while all the time, the gun sat in the Property Section of the Van Nuys division.

Three months after the murders, which had been separately pursued by the LAPD and the LA Sheriff's Office, neither group had made any progress. However, the detectives working for the Sheriff's Office were younger and more aggressive than their LAPD counterparts and came to the conclusion that the Tate and LaBianca cases were definitely connected. They had several suspects, one of which was Charles Manson.

The Spahn Ranch

The Spahn Ranch

Finally in mid-October, the LAPD began to talk to the Sheriff's Office and decided to investigate similarities between the murder of Gary Hinman and the Tate-LaBianca crimes. The investigation leads to the Spahn Ranch, which was the home of a hippie group that called itself the Manson Family.

The Spahn Ranch was in the mountains near Chatsworth. In the 1920's it had been the site for old cowboy movies. Author John Gilmore in his book *The Garbage People* describes the isolated old movie set:

The façade of the main street, a cluster of rundown movie buildings, had become a ghost town with its Longhorn Saloon, the Rock City Café, some stables, weathered props and old trailers. Millions of moviegoers once viewed this old "Wild West" setting, but the dust had settled. Rusted car parts littered the grounds and few visitors passed by...

Bobby Beausoleil, the man charged with the murder of Gary Hinman, had lived at the Spahn Ranch with the Manson Family.

His 17-year-old girlfriend told police that Manson sent Bobby and a girl named Susan Atkins to Hinman's house to get money from him. When Hinman wouldn't give them the money, they killed him. She also recalled that Susan Atkins mentioned a fight with a man who she stabbed in the legs several times.

When police questioned Susan Atkins, who was still in jail, she admitted that she went with Beausoleil to Hinman's home to get some money he had inherited. When he refused, Beausoleil slashed his face. The two of them kept Hinman prisoner in his home until Beausoleil murdered him a couple of days later.

At that point there did not seem to be any direct connection between Beausoleil and the Tate-LaBianca murders, except for some hearsay that Susan Atkins had stabbed a man in the leg. Gary Hinman had not been stabbed in the leg, but Voytek Frykowski had.

Susan Atkins

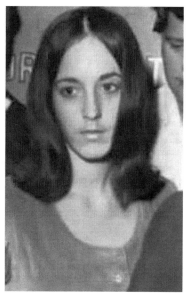

Susan Atkins

While she was awaiting trial for the murder of Gary Hinman, Susan Atkins was placed in the Sybil Brand Institute, L.A.'s women's house of detention. Her bed was next to that of 31-year-old Ronnie Howard. Another inmate, Virginia Graham, was a close friend of Ronnie's. Susan Atkins was a real talker. She had an almost unbelievable story that Ronnie and Virginia listened to with absolute amazement.

Atkins acted like a nut case: dancing and singing at the oddest times, oblivious to the seriousness of the charges against her and bubbling over with laughter and delight without any apparent reason.

In the course of conversation, Susan told Virginia that she was in for first degree murder.

"Did you do it?" Virginia wanted to know.

"Sure," Susan answered as though it were the most natural response in the world. But, the police thought that she only held Hinman while Bob Beausoleil stabbed him. In reality, Susan said, it was she who stabbed Hinman while Beausoleil held him.

She also told Virginia that her lover Charlie was Jesus Christ and he was going to lead her to a hole in the earth in Death Valley where there was a civilization down there. After hearing that story, Virginia was convinced that Atkins was completely nuts.

Several days later on November 6, Susan was again in a talky mood and mentioned the Sharon Tate murder. "You know who did it don't you?"

Confession

Virginia said she didn't.

"Well, you're looking at her."

Virginia was horrified and asked why she did such a thing.

"Because we wanted to do a crime that would shock the world that the world would have to stand up and take notice."

Atkins went on to explain that they selected the Tate house because it was isolated. Susan said they knew who the owner was but they didn't know or care who would be at the house that night.

Susan explained that there were four of them, three girls and a man, all of whom had been given their instructions by Charlie. When they got to the gate, the man cut the telephone wires. Next they shot the teenager four times because he had seen them.

When they got in the house, Susan said that in the living room there was a man on the couch and a woman on the chair reading. Then some of Susan's group stayed in the living room, while Susan went into the bedroom where Sharon was sitting on the bed talking to Jay Sebring. They quickly put nooses over Sharon and Jay's heads so that if they moved they would choke.

Frykowski ran for the door. "He was full of blood," she said and claimed that she had stabbed him three or four times. "He was bleeding and he ran to the front part, and would you believe that he was there hollering 'Help, help, somebody please help me,' and nobody came? Then we finished him off."

"Sharon was the last to die," Susan said with a laugh as she described how Sharon was begging her, "Please don't kill me. Please don't kill me. I don't want to die. I want to live. I want to have my baby. I want to have my baby."

Susan said she just looked at Sharon straight in the eye and said, "Look, bitch, I don't care about you. I don't care if you're going to have a baby. You had better be ready. You're going to die and I don't feel anything about it...In a few minutes I killed her."

Susan said she saw that there was Sharon's blood on her hand and she tasted it. "Wow, what a trip! To taste death, and yet give life."

Flabbergasted, Virginia asked Susan if it didn't bother her to kill a pregnant woman.

"I thought you understood. I loved her, and in order for me to kill her I was killing part of myself when I killed her," Susan explained. She had wanted to cut out Sharon's baby but there wasn't enough time. She had also wanted to take out all the victims' eyes and squash them against the walls and cut off and mutilate all of their fingers, but they didn't have the chance.

Susan told Virginia that after they left the Tate house she realized that she didn't have her knife with her any more. Not only that, she had left her palm print on a desk, "but my spirit was so strong that obviously it didn't even show up or they would have me by now." The four of them drove to a place where they were able to wash their hands and change their clothes.

The Plan

Susan ended the story with admitting that they killed the LaBianca's the next night. "That's part of the plan," she explained. "And there's more."

This tale of murder had Virginia's head spinning. She told Ronnie Howard, who didn't believe the story. "She's making it all up. She could have gotten it out of the papers," Ronnie reasoned. Virginia came up with a way to test Susan about whether she was telling the truth.

Some years earlier when the Tate house had been up for lease, Virginia had actually been to see the exterior of the house on Cielo drive. When she saw Susan, she asked her if the house was still decorated in gold and white. Susan said no.

Virginia also picked up some miscellaneous pieces of information that tied Charlie and Susan to that house. It used to belong to Terry Melcher, Doris Day's son. Charlie and Susan were angry with Melcher for some reason that was not clear. She babbled something about Melcher being too interested in money.

Later that day, Susan began to talk again and gave Virginia the list of celebrity targets that were next on their list: Richard Burton and Elizabeth Taylor, Frank Sinatra, Steve McQueen and Tom Jones. It was important to select victims that would shock the world.

She had planned to carve the words "helter skelter" on Elizabeth Taylor's face with a red-hot knife and then gouge her eyes out. Then she would castrate Richard Burton and put his penis along with Elizabeth Taylor's eyes in a bottle and mail it to Eddie Fisher.

Sinatra was to be skinned alive, while he listened to his own music. The Family would then make purses out of his skin and sell them in hippie shops. Tom Jones would have his throat slit, but only after being forced to have sex with Susan Atkins.

More Confessions

People who knew them but were not part of the group reported other confessions from Manson and Family members about the same time. On November 12, the L.A. Sheriff's detectives had a chance to interview Al Springer who was a member of the motorcycle gang called the Straight Satans who had been involved with the Manson Family off and on.

The detectives were astonished when Springer told them that a few days after the Tate murders that Manson had bragged to him about killing people: "We knocked off five of them just the other night." Springer stayed clear of Manson after that, but mentioned that Danny DeCarlo, another member of the motorcycle gang lived at the Spahn Ranch with the Family.

Springer and DeCarlo

In the course of the interview Springer asked if anyone had their refrigerator wrote on? "Charlie said they wrote something on the fucking refrigerator in blood...Something about pigs or niggers or something like that."

When the police finally got to Danny DeCarlo, they really got an earful about Charlie and his Family. Not only did DeCarlo confirm their culpability in Gary Hinman's death, but he implicated them in the death of a 36-year-old ranch hand named Shorty, a nickname for Donald Shea. He was killed because he'd tell the owner of the Spahn Ranch what was really happening on his property. "Shorty was going to tell old man Spahn...and Charlie didn't like snitches," DeCarlo explained.

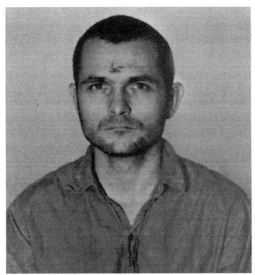

Bruce Davis

DeCarlo had been told what they did to his friend Shorty: "they stuck him like carving up a Christmas turkey...Bruce (Davis) said they cut him up in nine pieces. They cut his head off. Then they cut his arms off too, so there was no way they could possibly identify him. They were laughing about that."

Another Family member named Clem told DeCarlo with a big grin that "we got five piggies" the day after the Tate murders.

The two detectives shared this information with the detectives at the LAPD, but the latter did nothing with the information. The L.A. Sheriff's detectives, on the other hand, now focused their investigation on the Manson family believing that the hippie cult was somehow tied into both the Tate and LaBianca murder cases.

At some point in mid-November, Susan Atkins told her story to Ronnie Howard. Ronnie Howard felt that she had to tell the police about what Susan had revealed, especially since other people were future targets of the group. She asked for permission to contact LAPD, but was repeatedly denied, even though the woman she asked permission was dating one of the Tate case homicide detectives. Virginia Graham, who had been transferred to another facility, was running into the same kind of difficulty when she tried to tell the authorities about Susan.

Finally on November 17, 1969, two LAPD homicide detectives came to Sybil Brand to interview Ronnie Howard. The message was finally beginning to penetrate the collective intelligence of the LAPD that they had just found a gold mine. After they interviewed her, they had her moved for her safety into an isolation unit.

Charlie Manson

Just who was this Charlie anyway? Both the LAPD and the Los Angeles Sheriff's Office started to dig through the rubble of his heavily documented 36 years. As information came in about him, it was no surprise that he was in trouble. If ever a kid had a miserable start in life Charles Manson was it.

Little Charles Manson with his cousin (and possibly grandmother).

An illegitimate and unplanned child, he was born in Cincinnati, Ohio, November 12, 1934 to Kathleen Maddox, a promiscuous sixteen-year-old who drank too much and got into a lot of trouble. Two years later, Kathleen filed suit against Colonel Scott of Ashland, KY, for child support, which she was awarded, but never received. Kathleen was briefly married to William Manson who gave his name to the boy.

Charles Manson in Nuel Emmons' book *Manson in His Own Words* describes the Maddox family:

Kathleen was the youngest of three children from the marriage of Nancy and Charles Maddox. Her parents loved her and meant well by her, but they were fanatical in their religious beliefs. Especially Grandma, who dominated the household. She was stern and unwavering in her interpretation of God's Will, and demanded that those within her home abide by her view of God's wishes.

My grandfather worked for the B&O Railroad. He worked long hard hours, a dedicated slave to the company and his bosses...He was not the disciplinarian Grandma was...If he tried to comfort Mom with a display of affection, such as a pat on the knee or an arm around her shoulder, Grandma was quick to insinuate he was vulgar.

For Mom, life was filled with a never-ending list of denials. From awakening in the morning until going to bed at night it was, "No Kathleen, that dress is too short. Braid your hair; don't comb it like some hussy. Come directly home from school; don't let me catch you talking to any boys. No, you can't go to the school dance; we are going to church..." In 1933, at age fifteen, my mother ran away from home.

Other writers have portrayed Mom as a teenage whore...In her search for acceptance she may have fallen in love too easily and too often, but a whore at that time? No!...In later years, because of hard knocks and tough times, she may have sold her body some...

Charlie never knew his father and never had a real father figure. His mother was the kind that children are taken away from and placed in foster homes. Kathleen had a habit of disappearing for days and weeks at a time, leaving Charlie with his grandmother or his aunt. When Kathleen and her brother were both sentenced to the penitentiary for armed robbery, Charlie got sent off to live with his aunt and uncle in McMechen, West Virginia. The aunt was very religious and strict in stark contrast to his mother's permissiveness.

When Kathleen was released from jail, she was not responsible enough to take care of him, preferring her life of promiscuity and hard drinking to any kind of normal lifestyle. There was no continuity in his life: he was always being foisted on someone new; he moved from one dingy rooming house to another; there were only transitory friendships that he made on the streets.

Manson Sold for a Pitcher of Beer

Manson tells the story that circulated within his family: "Mom was in a café one afternoon with me on her lap. The waitress, a would-be mother without a child of her own, jokingly told my Mom she'd buy me from her. Mom replied, 'A pitcher of beer and he's yours.' The waitress set up the beer; Mom stuck around long enough to finish it off and left the place without me. Several days later my uncle had to search the town for the waitress and take me home."

John Gilmore in his insightful book called *The Garbage People* describes how Charlie adapted to this life of emptiness and violence:

He kept to himself. Though friendless, his young mind bypassed the loneliness of his surroundings. He watched, listened, pretended his imaginative resources knew no limit. And he began to steal, as if to hold onto something that continually flew away. There was a consistency and permanency to the habit of stealing and it became easier. With everything transient, the thefts and goods he carried with him offered a sense of stability, a kind of reward. An object owned gave identity to an owner, an identity that had yet to be acknowledged.

Teen aged Charles Manson

When he was nine, he was caught stealing and sent to reform school and then later when he was twelve, he was caught stealing again and sent to the Gibault School for Boys in Terre Haute, Indiana, in 1947. He ran away less than a year later and tried to return to his mother who didn't want him. Living entirely by stealing and burglary, he lived on his own until he was caught. The court arranged for him to go to Father Flanagan's Boys Town.

He didn't last long at Boys Town. A few days after his arrival, thirteen-year-old Charlie and another kid committed two armed robberies. A few more episodes like that landed Charlie in the Indiana School for Boys for three years. His teachers described him as having trust in no one and "did good work only for those from whom he figured he could obtain something."

Institutional Politician

In 1951, Charlie and two other boys escaped and headed for California living entirely by burglary and auto theft. They got as far as Utah when they were caught. This time he was sent to the National Training School for Boys in Washington, D.C. While he was there they gave him various tests which established that his IQ was 109, that he was illiterate and that his aptitude for everything but music was average.

His keepers said this about him: "Manson has become somewhat of an 'institution politician.' He does just enough work to get by on. Restless and moody most of the time, the boy would rather spend his class time entertaining his friend. It appears that this boy is a very emotionally upset youth who is definitely in need of some psychiatric orientation."

That same year, Dr. Block, a psychiatrist examined him, noting "the marked degree of rejection, instability and psychic trauma." His illegitimacy, small physical size and lack of parental love caused him to constantly strive for status with the other boys. "This could add up to a fairly slick institutionalized youth," Dr. Block concluded, "but one is left with the feeling that behind all this lies an extremely sensitive boy who has not yet given up in terms of securing some kind of love and affection from the world."

For a short time, things started to look up for Charlie. His aunt had agreed to take care of him and his chances for parole were good. Shortly before the parole hearing, Charlie held a razor blade against another boy's throat while he sodomized him. Charlie was transferred to the Federal Reformatory at Petersburg, Virginia, where he was characterized as definitely homosexual, dangerous and safe only under supervision.

In September of 1952, he was sent to a more secure institution in Chillicothe, Ohio. His keepers there saw him as "criminally sophisticated despite his age and grossly unsuited for retention in an open reformatory type institution." For some reason, Manson suddenly changed his attitude. He was more cooperative and genuinely improved educationally so that he was able to read and understand basic math. This improvement leads to his parole in May of 1954 at the age of nineteen.

At first he lived with his aunt and uncle, then his mother for a short period of time. Early in 1955, he married a waitress who bore him a son, Charles Manson, Jr. Charlie worked at various low-paying jobs and augmented his income by stealing cars. One of them he took to Los Angeles with his then pregnant wife. Inevitably, he was caught again and eventually found his way to the prison at Terminal Island in San Pedro, California.

Charles Manson with his wife (Wedding Day)

1956 Mugshot

The Manipulator

His wife had the good sense to divorce him after he spent three years in jail. In 1958, he was released on parole. This time Manson took up a new occupation — pimping. He supplemented this income by getting money from an unattractive wealthy girl in Pasadena. In 1959, Manson was arrested on two federal charges: stealing a check from a mailbox and attempting to cash a U.S. Treasury check for $37.50

This time Manson was lucky, a young woman pretended she was pregnant and pleaded with the judge to keep him out of jail. The judge believed the story and had pity on him. While he sentenced Charlie to ten years, he then immediately placed him on probation. A couple of months later, he was arrested by the LAPD for stealing cars and using stolen credit cards, but the charges were dropped for lack of evidence.

Near the end of 1959, Manson conned a young woman out of $700 in savings to invest in his nonexistent company. To make matters worse, he got her pregnant and then drugged and raped her roommate. He fled to Texas but was arrested and put in prison to serve out his ten-year sentence. "If there ever was a man who demonstrated himself completely unfit for probation, he is it," the judge said. Eventually at the age of 26 he was sent to the U.S. Penitentiary at McNeil Island, Washington.

His record there described Charlie as having "a tremendous drive to call attention to himself. Generally he is unable to succeed in positive acts; therefore he often resorts to negative behavior to satisfy this drive. In his efforts to "find" himself, Manson peruses different religious philosophies, e.g. Scientology and Buddhism; however, he never remains long enough with any given teachings to reap meaningful benefits."

By 1964, he hadn't changed much, as least as viewed by prison officials: "His past pattern of employment instability continues...seems to have an intense need to call attention to himself...remains emotionally insecure and tends to involve himself in various fanatical interests."

Whatever those "fanatical" interests were, they included an obsession with the Beatles. Manson's guitar was another obsession. He felt that with the right opportunities he would be much bigger than the Beatles. In prison, he became friends with the aging gangster, Alvin Karpis. The former Public Enemy Number One and sole survivor of the Ma Barker gang taught Charlie how to play the steel guitar. The prison record noted in May of 1966 that "he has been spending most of his free time writing songs, accumulating about 80 or 90 of them during the past year...He also plays the guitar and drums, and is hopeful that he can secure employment as a guitar player or as a drummer or singer."

Karpis had some interesting insights into Charlie's true personality: "There was something unmistakably unusual about Manson. He was a runt of sorts, but found his place as an experienced manipulator of others. I did feel manipulated, and under circumstances where it hadn't been necessary."

On March 21, 1967, Charlie was released from prison and given transportation to San Francisco. He was 32 years old and more than half of his life had been spent in institutions. He protested his freedom. "Oh, no, I can't go outside there...I knew that I couldn't adjust to that world, not after all my life had been spent locked up and where my mind was free. I was content to stay in the penitentiary, just to take my walks around the yard in the sunshine and to play my guitar..." The prison officials ignored his protest and unleashed him on the world again.

Charlie's Followers
"The Manson Family"

As poorly prepared for life on the outside as he was, Charlie was able to blend in with his guitar into the hippie scene in San Francisco. The high-point of the Haight Ashbury culture was past and the only ones left were the diehards and the last ones to the party. Charlie was never impressed by the hippie culture, but he lived off it and it didn't expect much from him. He learned about drugs and how he could use them to influence people.

Charlie started to attract a group of followers, many of whom were very young women with troubled emotional lives who were rebelling against their parents and society in general. He battered down their inhibitions and questioned the validity of their notions of good and evil. For the most part, Charlie's followers were weak-willed people who were naïve, gullible and easy to lead. LSD and amphetamines were additional tools by which Charlie altered their personalities to his needs.

In spring of 1968, Manson and his followers left San Francisco in an old school bus and traveled around. Eventually, he and a few of his group moved in with Gary Hinman, a music teacher with a house on the Canyon Road. Through Hinman, Charlie met Dennis Wilson of the Beach Boys. Manson and his girls starting hanging around Wilson every chance they had. Manson tried to leverage the acquaintance with Dennis Wilson but it didn't go anywhere. Eventually, Wilson became uncomfortable with Manson and his girls and told them to split.

About that time, Manson found George Spahn and conned the old man into letting him and his followers live on the Ranch. Squeaky Fromme, one of Charlie's devotees, made sure that the elderly man's sexual needs were fully satisfied. The Manson Family survived by a combination of stealing and scavenging. Much of their food was taken from what the supermarkets discard each day.

Charlie was still hell-bent to market his music to somebody. Through his contacts with Dennis Wilson and another man in the music business, Charlie met Doris Day's son Terry Melcher. The plan was to interest Melcher in financing a film with Manson's music.

At that time, Melcher owned the house on Cielo Drive that was eventually leased to Roman Polanski and Sharon Tate. At various times, Manson had been by the property in a car with Dennis Wilson.

Melcher was asked to listen to Charlie and decide whether or not he wanted to record them. Melcher went out the first time and listened to Charlie sing his own compositions and play the guitar. Some of the girls sang and played tambourines. Melcher went out a second time a week later, but the music was nothing he was interested in recording. What he didn't realize is that Manson had built this recording opportunity with Melcher into something very real in his mind. When nothing came of it, Charlie was plenty angry and blamed Melcher for his disappointment.

Helter Skelter

Another facet of Charlie, although not nearly as important to him as his music, was his philosophy. To a large extent, this "philosophy" was a con, something he dreamed up to impress his followers, but he probably believed some of it.

The core of this philosophy was a kind of Armageddon. Charlie preached that the black man was going to rise up and start killing the whites and turn the cities in to an inferno of racial revenge. The black man would win this war, but wouldn't be able to hang onto the power he seized because of innate inferiority.

In 1968, Charlie was forecasting racial war when all of a sudden the Beatles released their White Album, which had the song "Helter Skelter." The lyrics fit Charlie's theory to a tee: "Look out helter skelter helter skelter helter skelter/She's coming down fast/ Yes she is/Yes she is." Now, the racial Armageddon had a name. It was Helter Skelter.

Helter Skelter would begin, according to one of Charlie's devotees, "with the black man going into white people's homes and ripping off the white people, physically destroying them. A couple of spades from Watts would come up into the Bel Air and Beverly Hills district...and just really wipe some people out, just cutting bodies up and smearing blood and writing things on the wall in blood...all kinds of super-atrocious crimes that would really make the white man mad...until there was open revolution in the streets, until they finally won and took over. Then the black man would assume the white man's karma. He would then be the establishment..."

Charlie and the Family would survive this racial holocaust because they would be hiding in the desert safe from the turmoil of the cities. He pulled from the Book of Revelations, the concept of a "bottomless pit," the entrance of which, according to Charlie, was a cave underneath Death Valley that led down to a city of gold. This paradise was where Charlie and his Family were going to wait out this war. Afterwards, when the black man failed at keeping power, Charlie's Family, which they estimated would have multiplied to 144,000 by that time, would then take over from the black man and rule the cities.

"It will be our world then," Charlie told his followers. "There would be no one else, except for us and the black servants. He, Charles Willis Manson, the fifth angel, Jesus Christ, would then rule the world. The other four angels were the Beatles.

How did this hokey philosophy result in the blood bath at the Tate and LaBianca houses? Well, Charlie the Prophet had already forecast that the murders would start in the summer of 1969, but as the summer went on, it looked as though the "prophet" was wrong. "The only thing blackie knows is what whitey has told him," he said to one of his followers just before the murders. "I'm going to have to show him how to do it."

After the LaBianca murder, one of Manson's girls, Linda Kasabian, was told to take Rosemary LaBianca's wallet and credit cards and leave them in the ladies room of a gas station in an area heavily populated by blacks. That way, when, theoretically, the credit cards would be used by some black woman, it would appear that blacks were responsible for the LaBianca deaths. However, the credit cards were never used or turned in to the authorities.

Prosecution

Vincent Bugliosi

On November 18, 1969, 35-year-old Deputy District Attorney Vincent T. Bugliosi was assigned the Tate-LaBianca murder cases. Aaron Stovitz, head of the Trials Division of the District Attorney's Office, was assigned as a co-prosecutor, but was later pulled off for another case.

Bugliosi had an unbelievably difficult job ahead of him. Not only did he need to prove that members of the Manson Family were responsible for the Tate and LaBianca murders, but he had to prove the Charles Manson ordered them to do it. While Manson had sent four Family members to the Cielo Drive massacre, he did not go himself. He did, however, tie up Rosemary and Leno LaBianca and gave three others instructions to kill them.

The prosecutor had to establish Charlie's dominance over the members of his Family and convince a jury that Charlie had sufficient motive to want these seven people dead.

Charles (Tex) Watson

At the beginning, he didn't have much of a case. There was Susan Atkins' story as related to Virginia Graham and the stories that Al Springer and Danny DeCarlo told the police, along with some comments from other people interviewed about Manson and his followers. It wasn't until December 3 that Bugliosi knew for certain who of Manson's Family had actually been involved with the murders. Manson had sent Charles "Tex" Watson, Susan Atkins, Patricia Krenwinkel, and Linda Kasabian to the Tate residence. Accompanying him to the LaBianca home was Watson, Krenwinkel, and Leslie Van Houten. Atkins, Kasabian and Steve "Clem" Grogan waited in the car.

Atkins' testimony was deemed vital to the prosecution, but she was not offered immunity. However, if she cooperated with the prosecution, they would not seek the death penalty against her in any of the three cases: Hinman, Tate and LaBianca. The extent to which she cooperated would affect whether the prosecution would press for first-degree murder, life sentence, etc.

Things started to look up for the prosecution when a fingerprint of Patricia Krenwinkel's was found on a door inside of Sharon Tate's bedroom. This physical evidence was added to the .22 caliber bullets found at the Spahn Ranch (the gun used at the Tate murders was a .22 caliber revolver).

The first order of business for Bugliosi was to get grand jury indictments against Manson and the individuals involved in the murders. When Susan Atkins testified to the grand jury, she gave the same bloodcurdling story to them that she gave to Ronnie Howard and Virginia Graham. She showed absolutely no sign of guilt or remorse for the ghastly things she did. The jurors stared at her in disbelief.

Biker Danny DeCarlo testified that he, Manson, Watson and others had used a .22 caliber Buntline revolver for target practice at the Spahn Ranch.

He also said that the three-strand nylon rope that was used in the Tate murders was identical to the rope used at the ranch.

Linda Kasabian

It only took the grand jury twenty minutes to hand down the indictments Bugliosi sought: Charles Manson, Charles "Tex" Watson, Patricia Krenwinkel, Susan Atkins, and Linda Kasabian, seven counts of murder and one count of conspiracy to commit murder; Leslie van Houten, two counts of murder and one count of conspiracy to commit murder.

Evidence

A few days later, the wallet belonging to Rosemary LaBianca was found in the ladies restroom at the service station where Linda Kasabian left it. The wallet had gotten lodged in the toilet tank. This piece of corroborating evidence was necessary to bolster Susan Atkins' story in case she decided to repudiate her testimony when Charlie started to pressure her.

Another critical piece of evidence was finally "found:" the unusual .22 caliber Hi Standard Longhorn revolver with the broken gun grip which had been found by Bernard Weiss' son and turned over to the police three and a half months earlier. Bernard Weiss after reading about the indictments in the newspaper called LAPD Homicide to see if the revolver he had turned in was the murder weapon.

After being passed around to several people, an officer told Weiss "We don't keep guns that long. We throw them in the ocean after a while."

Weiss said, "I can't believe that you'd throw away what could be the single most important piece of evidence in the Tate case."

Leslie Van Houten

"Listen, mister," was the official answer. "We can't check out every citizen report on every gun we find."

Weiss called a newscaster, who in turn, called the LAPD. The gun was "found" where it had been "lost" in the Van Nuys police station. After the tests had been run, there was no doubt that it was the murder weapon. One thing remained to be done — linking Manson to that particular revolver. Eventually Randy Starr provided that link. He once owned the revolver and had given it to Manson.

Another important development occurred when the police were contacted by the man who owned the place that the Tate killers had used to clean up right after the murders. The man had remembered the car and the license plate, which was traced to a Spahn Ranch employee, who had let Manson and his girls borrow his car.

Motive

Manson mugshot

Even though it was not necessary for the prosecution to establish the motive for the crimes, Bugliosi considered motive an important piece of evidence, especially since Manson was not physically present at the Tate murders. Bugliosi set out to establish that the primary motive was Helter Skelter: Manson's belief that he could start a race war and personally gain from it. But certainly, there was the connection between Manson's anger at Terry Melcher and the crimes committed on his former property. To further bolster that motive, it was established that two different people had chased Manson off the property a few months before the murders.

Rudi Altobelli, the man who bought the Cielo Drive property from Melcher, was an important man in the entertainment industry. He represented stars like Katherine Hepburn and Henry Fonda. Because he traveled so much, he rented out the property to the Polanski's and stayed in the guesthouse when he visited the area.

In March of 1969, Manson went to the house where four of the five murdered people were staying. Charlie said he was looking for Melcher. Sharon's houseguest sent him away in not too friendly terms, but not before he saw Sharon, who wondered what the "creepy looking guy" wanted.

Then Manson went to the guesthouse and told Rudi Altobelli that the people in the main house told him to ask at the guesthouse. Altobelli admonished Manson for bothering his tenants and told him he didn't know where Terry Melcher had moved.

Manson knew the layout of the house and he knew who was living in it. It was quite possible that the "Helter Skelter" crimes were committed at that particular house because Charlie wanted to pay back the residents for rejecting him and scare the daylights out of Melcher for not backing his recording career.

Manson himself became a major player as he appeared frequently in the courtroom. Bugliosi studied him and described the behavior he witnessed:

Though he had little formal schooling, he was fairly articulate, and definitely bright. He picked up little nuances, seemed to consider all of the hidden sides of a question before answering. His moods were mercurial, his facial expressions chameleon-like. Underneath, however, there was a strange intensity. You felt it even when he was joking, which, despite the seriousness of the charges, was often. He frequently played to the always-packed courtroom, not only to the Family faithful but to the press and spectators as well. Spotting a pretty girl, he'd often smile or wink. Usually they appeared more flattered than offended.

The Trial

The trial officially began in mid-June of 1970. Judge Charles Older presided. He decided that the jury, once selected, would be locked up until the end of the trial — "to protect them from harassment and to prevent their being exposed to trial publicity." Older was given a bodyguard and his home was provided with protection.

The twelve jurors selected were five women and seven men with a range of ages spanning from 25 to 73. While many occupations were represented, one was a retired deputy sheriff.

In his opening statement, Bugliosi characterized Manson as "vagrant wanderer, a frustrated singer-guitarist...who would refer to himself as Jesus Christ...and was a killer who cleverly masqueraded behind the common image of a hippie that of being peace loving...but was a megalomaniac who coupled his insatiable thirst for power with an intense obsession for violent death."

Bugliosi stressed that Manson commanded his followers to commit the murders, but that "the evidence will show that they were very willing participants in these mass murders..."

Manson, who first appeared to the jury with a bloody X that he had carved into his forehead, insisted on defending himself. He was assisted by an older lawyer named Irving Kanarek, who was legendary for his attention to detail (much to the frustration of witnesses, judges and juries) and Ronald Hughes, "the hippie lawyer" who was Leslie Van Houten's attorney.

Critical to Manson's defense was maintaining control of the Family. If his followers testified against him, he was doomed. He had to set up and maintain an effective communications network between himself and the other Family members, particularly those under indictment. He needed the Family members who were not in jail to communicate his wishes to those who were.

Just how sinister this communication would be was evidenced by what happened to Barbara Hoyt. Hoyt was one of the prosecution's witnesses, who was threatened that if she testified at the trial, she and her family would be killed. She was then lured to Honolulu by one of Manson's girls and given a lethal dose of LSD. Fortunately, she got to the hospital in time for doctors to save her.

Manson was able to exert a lot of control over his girls in the courtroom. By then Susan Atkins had repudiated her testimony to the grand jury. They came up with bizarre stories that would implicate themselves but spare their beloved Charlie.

As the evidence was presented, things were looking bad for Charlie and the girls. A pattern was developing, according to Bugliosi: "The more damaging the testimony, the more chance that Manson would create a disturbance, thereby assuring that he — and not the evidence itself — would get the day's headlines. Often these disturbances would result in Judge Older removing them from the courtroom.

The drama hit a high point when Manson got into an argument with Judge Older and jumped towards the judge, yelling, "someone should cut your head off!" Atkins, Krenwinkel and Van Houten stood up and started chanting in Latin.

When Manson and his girls were removed from the court, a shaken Judge Older instructed the jury to disregard what they heard and saw, but the effect was indelible. The jury got a first hand chance to see the real Charles Manson.

After 22 weeks of trial, the Prosecution rested. It was time for the defense attorneys to do their part. Judge Older told the lawyers that were assisting Manson and defending the girls to call their first witness. The defense responded: "Thank you, Your Honor. The defendants rest."

The court was stunned. Then the three girls shouted that they wanted to testify. The judge and everyone else was bewildered. The girls had decided that they would testify that *they* planned and committed the murders themselves and that Charlie had nothing to do with it.

Ronald Hughes, Leslie Van Houten's "hippie lawyer" objected and stood up against Manson's transparent ploy: "I refuse to take part in any proceeding where I am forced to push a client out the window." A few days later, Ronald Hughes had disappeared. After the trial was over, his body was found wedged between two boulders in Ventura County. One of Manson's followers later admitted that the Manson Family had murdered him.

A new lawyer had to be found immediately to take over the defense. Maxwell Keith was appointed. When the court reconvened, Manson and the girls created a disturbance suggesting that Judge Older "did away with Ronald Hughes," which resulted in them being removed again from the courtroom.

For the most part, the lawyers for the defense put forth a disappointing presentation. Paul Fitzgerald, Patricia Krenwinkel's attorney, spent more time defending Manson than his client. Daye Shinn, Susan Atkins' lawyer made a brief defense for his client. Irving Kanarek went on for days in his rambling style. Finally, Judge Older accused him of filibustering. Manson, apparently also tired of Kanarek's exhausting argument, shouted at him: "Why don't you sit down? You're just making things worse."

Verdict

Vanhouten, Atkin and Krenwinkel return to court

On January 15, 1971, seven months after the start of the trial, the jury began to deliberate. Nine days later, it came to a verdict. Security was very tight around the Hall of Justice since a Manson follower had stolen a case of hand grenades from a Marine Base and reportedly had planned a special event on what they were calling "Judgment Day."

The jury had found Charles Manson, Patricia Krenwinkel, Susan Atkins and Leslie Van Houten each guilty of murder and conspiracy to commit murder.

Charles "Tex" Watson, because of extradition proceedings and other legal complications did not stand trial until later in the year and was also found guilty of murder and conspiracy to commit murder.

Manson Girls shave their heads after Manson verdict

On March 29, 1971, the jury completed deliberations on the penalty phase of the trial. Manson and the three female defendants had shaved their heads for the reading of their verdicts.

"We, the jury in the above-entitled action, having found the defendant Charles Manson guilty of murder in the first degree...do now fix the penalty as death."

Patricia Krenwinkel responded: "You have just judged yourselves."

"Better lock your doors and watch your own kids," Susan Atkins said.

All four defendants received the death penalty.

On April 19, 1971, Superior Court Judge Charles H. Older pronounced the judgment: "It is my considered judgment that not only is the death penalty appropriate, but it is almost compelled by the circumstances. I must agree with the prosecutor that if this is not a proper case for the death penalty, what should be?"

The judge shook the hands of each juror. "If it were within the power of a trial judge to award a medal of honor to jurors, believe me, I would bestow an award on each of you."

At a later date, Robert Beausoleil, Charles Manson, Charles Watson, Bruce Davis and Steve Grogan were tried and convicted for the murders of Gary Hinman and Donald (Shorty) Shea.

Bugliosi wrote," it had been the longest murder trial in American history, lasting nine and a half months; the most expensive, costing approximately $1 million; and the most highly publicized; while the jury had been sequestered 225 days, longer than any jury before it. The trial transcript alone ran to 209 volumes, 31,716 pages, approximately eight million words."

In 1972, the California Supreme Court abolished the death penalty in the state and all of the defendants are serving life sentences.

Afterward

Right after the trial, there were a number of articles written that were favorable to Manson and his followers. For a while, it appeared that he might become some sort of cult hero. That never really materialized, however, and there is very little left of the Manson Family today. However, Manson still receives a large amount of mail, much of it from young people who want to join the Family.

Lynette Fromme

There have been several plays about him, movies and documentaries and even an opera. Charlie's music has been played by the Guns N' Roses rock band.

Why, when other murderers that were responsible for many more deaths than Manson are forgotten by most people, does Manson remain so notorious?

Perhaps because the people they murdered and the ones they planned to murder were celebrities. Also, perhaps because of Lynette "Squeaky" Fromme's failed attempt to assassinate President Gerald Ford in 1975, even though it is unlikely that Manson put her up to it.

Bugliosi believes the notoriety continues because it is the most bizarre and strange, almost unbelievable, murder case in history. He thinks that Manson has become a "metaphor" for evil, catapulting him to near mythological proportions...People worry about this man the way they worry about cancer and earthquakes."

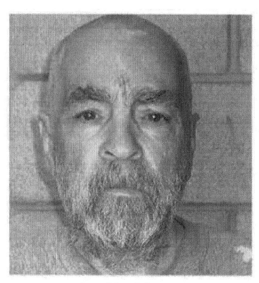

An older Manson

Manson endures, even as a sixty-year old, comparatively passive prisoner, unlikely to ever be paroled. Bugliosi sums up the continued fascination with the more fanatical elements of society: "Today, almost every disaffected and morally twisted group in America, from Satanists to neo-Nazi skinheads, has embraced Manson and the poisons of his virulent philosophy. He has become their spiritual icon, the high priest of anti-establishment hatred."

Where Are They Now?

Charles Manson

Charles Manson Then

Charles Manson Now

In 1989, Nikolas Schreck conducted an interview of Manson, cutting the interview up for material in his documentary *Charles Manson Superstar*. This was the first, and is considered one of the most authoritative and comprehensive, documentaries on the subject. Schreck concluded that the story behind the murders was probably false, and that an admitted plan, by several of the women at the ranch interviewed after the trial was concluded, involved killing the people at the Tate home in order to free Bobby Beausoleil as per an attempt to copycat the murder of Gary Hinman. According to this, the use of writings of blood on the walls at the Tate and LaBianca residences was merely a ploy to make it seem that the murderer of Hinman was still free, and that Beausoleil was not guilty. Key in his refutation of the hypothesis was the fact that, while the prosecution attempted to show Manson ordered the killings because he was upset over Terry Melcher (and believed Melcher to still be at that address), this could certainly not have been the case, as Manson attempted on several occasions to contact Melcher at his new address, showing he knew very well Melcher no longer lived at the Tate home. Schreck also concluded that Manson was not insane, but merely acting that way out of frustration.

On September 25, 1984, while imprisoned at the California Medical Facility at Vacaville, Manson was severely burned by a fellow inmate who poured paint thinner on him and set him alight. The other prisoner, Jan Holmstrom, explained that Manson had objected to his Hare Krishna chants and had verbally threatened him. Despite suffering second- and third-degree burns over 20 percent of his body, Manson recovered from his injuries. In December 1987, Fromme, serving a life sentence for the assassination attempt, escaped briefly from Alderson Federal Prison Camp in West Virginia. She was trying to reach Manson, who she had heard had testicular cancer; she was apprehended within days. She was released on parole from Federal Medical Center, Carswell on August 14, 2009.

Later events

In a 1994 conversation with Manson prosecutor Vincent Bugliosi, Catherine Share, a one-time Manson-follower, stated that her testimony in the penalty phase of Manson's trial had been a fabrication intended to save Manson from the gas chamber and had been given on Manson's explicit direction. Share's testimony had introduced the copycat-motive story, which the testimony of the three female defendants echoed and according to which the Tate-LaBianca murders had been Linda Kasabian's idea. In a 1997 segment of the tabloid television program *Hard Copy*, Share implied that her testimony had been given under a Manson threat of physical harm. In August 1971, after Manson's trial and sentencing, Share had participated in a violent California retail store robbery, the object of which was the acquisition of weapons to help free Manson.

In January 1996, a Manson website was established by latter-day Manson follower George Stimson, who was helped by Sandra Good. Good had been released from prison in 1985, after serving 10 years of her 15-year sentence for the death threats. The Manson website, ATWA.com, was discontinued in 2001, but as of 2011, it was running again, but currently the domain is up for sale and the website is discontinued.

In June 1997, Manson was found to have been trafficking in drugs by a prison disciplinary committee. That August, he was moved from Corcoran State Prison to Pelican Bay State Prison.

In a 1998–99 interview in *Seconds* magazine, Bobby Beausoleil rejected the view that Manson ordered him to kill Gary Hinman. He stated Manson did come to Hinman's house and slash Hinman with a sword. In a 1981 interview with *Oui* magazine, he denied this. Beausoleil stated that when he read about the Tate murders in the newspaper, "I wasn't even sure at that point – really, I had no idea who had done it until Manson's group were actually arrested for it. It had only crossed my mind and I had a premonition, perhaps. There was some little tickle in my mind that the killings might be connected with them ..." In the *Oui* magazine interview, he had stated, "When the Tate-LaBianca murders happened, I knew who had done it. I was fairly certain."

William Garretson, once the young caretaker at Cielo Drive, indicated in a program broadcast in July 1999 on *E!*, that he had, in fact, seen and heard a portion of the Tate murders from his location in the property's guest house. This comported with the unofficial results of the polygraph examination that had been given to Garretson on August 10, 1969, and that had effectively eliminated him as a suspect. The LAPD officer who conducted the examination had concluded Garretson was "clean" on participation in the crimes but "muddy" as to his having heard anything. Garretson did not explain why he had withheld his knowledge of the events.

Later developments

Manson at age 74 (March 2009)

On September 5, 2007, MSNBC aired *The Mind of Manson*, a complete version of a 1987 interview at California's San Quentin State Prison. The footage of the "unshackled, unapologetic, and unruly" Manson had been considered "so unbelievable" that only seven minutes of it had originally been broadcast on *The Today Show*, for which it had been recorded.

In a January 2008 segment of the Discovery Channel's *Most Evil*, Barbara Hoyt said that the impression that she had accompanied Ruth Ann Moorehouse to Hawaii just to avoid testifying at Manson's trial was erroneous. Hoyt said she had cooperated with the Family because she was "trying to keep them from killing my family." She stated that, at the time of the trial, she was "constantly being threatened: 'Your family's gonna die. The murders could be repeated at your house.'"

On March 15, 2008, the Associated Press reported that forensic investigators had conducted a search for human remains at Barker Ranch the previous month. Following up on longstanding rumors that the Family had killed hitchhikers and runaways who had come into its orbit during its time at Barker, the investigators identified "two likely clandestine grave sites ... and one additional site that merits further investigation." Though they recommended digging, CNN reported on March 28 that the Inyo County sheriff, who questioned the methods they employed with search dogs, had ordered additional tests before any excavation. On May 9, after a delay caused by damage to test equipment, the sheriff announced that test results had been inconclusive and that "exploratory excavation" would begin on May 20. In the meantime, Tex Watson had commented publicly that "no one was killed" at the desert camp during the month-and-a-half he was there, after the Tate-LaBianca murders. On May 21, after two days of work, the sheriff brought the search to an end; four potential gravesites had been dug up and had been found to hold no human remains. In March 2009, a photograph taken of a 74-year old Manson, showing a receding hairline, grizzled gray beard and hair and the swastika tattoo still prominent on his forehead, was released to the public by California corrections officials.

In September 2009, The History Channel broadcast a docudrama covering the Family's activities and the murders as part of its coverage on the 40th anniversary of the killings. The program included an in-depth interview with Linda Kasabian, who spoke publicly for the first time since a 1989 appearance on *A Current Affair*, an American television news magazine. Also included in the History Channel program were interviews with Vincent Bugliosi, Catherine Share, and Debra Tate, sister of Sharon.

As the 40th anniversary of the Tate-LaBianca murders approached, in July 2009, *Los Angeles* magazine published an "oral history", in which former Family members, law-enforcement officers, and others involved with Manson, the arrests, and the trials offered their recollections of—and observations on—the events that made Manson notorious. In the article, Juan Flynn, a Spahn Ranch worker who had become associated with Manson and the Family, said, "Charles Manson got away with everything. People will say, 'He's in jail.' But Charlie is exactly where he wants to be."

In November 2009, a Los Angeles DJ and songwriter named Matthew Roberts released correspondence and other evidence indicating he had been biologically fathered by Manson. Roberts' biological mother claims to have been a member of the Manson Family who left in the summer of 1967 after being raped by Manson; the mother returned to her parents' home to complete the pregnancy, gave birth on March 22, 1968, and subsequently gave up Roberts for adoption. Manson himself has stated that he "could" be the father, acknowledging the biological mother and a sexual relationship with her during 1967; this was nearly two years before the Family began its murderous phase.

In 2010, the *Los Angeles Times* reported that Manson was caught with a cell phone in 2009, and had contacted people in California, New Jersey, Florida and British Columbia. A spokesperson for the California Department of Corrections stated that it was not known if Manson had used the phone for criminal purposes.

On October 4, 2012, Bruce Davis, who had been convicted of the murder of Shorty Shea and the attempted robbery by Manson Family members of a Hawthorne gun shop in 1971, was recommended for parole by the California Department of Corrections at his 27th parole hearing. In 2010, Governor Arnold Schwarzenegger had reversed the board's previous finding in favor of Davis, denying him parole for two more years. On March 1, 2013, Governor Jerry Brown also denied parole for Davis.

Parole hearings

Manson at age 76 in June 2011

A footnote to the conclusion of *California v. Anderson*, the 1972 decision that neutralized California's then-current death sentences, stated, "Any prisoner now under a sentence of death ... may file a petition for writ of habeas corpus in the superior court inviting that court to modify its judgment to provide for the appropriate alternative punishment of life imprisonment or life imprisonment without possibility of parole specified by statute for the crime for which he was sentenced to death." This made Manson eligible to apply for parole after seven years' incarceration. His first parole hearing took place on November 16, 1978, at the California Medical Facility in Vacaville.

Manson was denied parole for the 12th time on April 11, 2012. Manson did not attend the hearing where prison officials argued that Manson had a history of controlling behavior and mental health issues including schizophrenia and paranoid delusional disorder and was too great a danger to be released. It was determined that Manson would not be reconsidered for parole for another 15 years, at which time he would be 92 years old.

His California Department of Corrections and Rehabilitation inmate number at Corcoran State Prison is B33920.

Charles Manson, 79, to marry girlfriend 'Star,' 25?

She says yes; he says 'garbage'

Murderer Manson is still doing life in Corcoran Prison for the Tate-LaBianca slayings — His girlfriend wants the world to know that he is her 'husband.'

Charles Manson is to marry his 25-year-old girlfriend behind bars, she has claimed.

In an interview with Rolling Stone magazine, the young woman who calls herself "Star," tells the world that she is to be the next bride of the 79-year-old.

"I'll tell you straight up, Charlie and I are going to get married," she told Rolling Stone magazine. "When that will be, we don't know. But I take it very seriously. Charlie is my husband. Charlie told me to tell you this. We haven't told anybody about that.

"People can think I'm crazy. But they don't know. This is what's right for me. This is what I was born for," she told the magazine. The pair has been in a relationship since "Star" was 19.

She began visiting him at Corcoran State Prison in California when she was still a teenager. She is originally from Missouri.

"Star" has even cut an "X" into her forehead, in an apparent twisted homage to Mason's swastika symbol.

Manson has been incarcerated for 44 years since the cult leader was convicted of the murders of actress Sharon Tate and Leno and Rosemary LaBianco.

Manson, who has been married twice before, denied the claim of marriage.

"That's a bunch of garbage. You know that, man. That's trash. We're just playing that for public consumption," he told Rolling Stone. He also revealed that he was bisexual.

Manson said: "Sex to me is like going to the toilet. Whether it's a girl or not, it doesn't matter."

Star began visiting Manson at Corcoran State Prison in California when she was still a teenager.

Charles Manson with Star, who says they are to marry. But Manson says, "That's a bunch of garbage. You know that, man. That's trash. We're just playing that for public consumption."

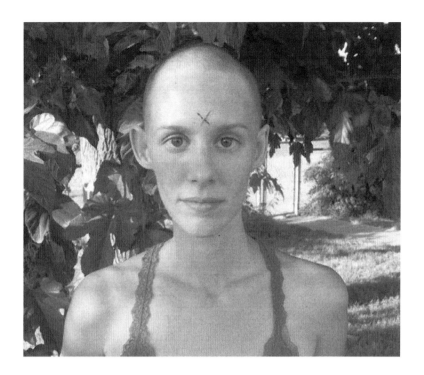

Star said in Rolling Stone magazine, "I'll tell you straight up, Charlie and I are going to get married."

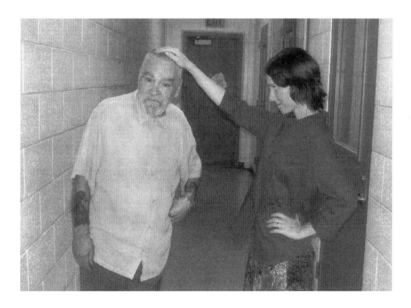

Star says of her relationship with Manson, "this is what's right for me. This is what I was born for."

Leslie Van Houten

Leslie Van Houten Then

Leslie Van Houten Now

Former Charles Manson follower Leslie Van Houten was denied parole June 5, 2013 for the 20th time.

Van Houten, 63, told a California parole board in unprecedented detail how committed she was to the murders Manson ordered and asserted she has changed and is trying to live a life of healing.

But Board of Parole Hearings Commissioner Jeffrey Ferguson told Van Houten she had failed to explain how someone as intelligent and well-bred as she was could have committed the "cruel and atrocious" murders of Leno and Rosemary La Bianca, and the panel rejected her bid.

Van Houten will be eligible for another parole hearing in five years.

"I know I did something that is unforgiveable, but I can create a world where I make amends," Van Houten said. "I'm trying to be someone who lives a life for healing rather than destruction."

The panel was also heard from relatives of the victims who were starkly opposed to her parole.

"There are certain crimes that are so heinous, so atrocious, so horrible that it should cause denial of parole."

— L.A. County Deputy District Attorney Patrick Sequiera

Van Houten was convicted of murder and conspiracy for her role in the slayings of wealthy Los Angeles grocers Leno and Rosemary La Bianca. They were stabbed to death in August 1969, one night after Manson's followers killed actress Sharon Tate and four others.

Van Houten did not participate in the Tate killings but went along the next night when the La Bianca's were slain in their home. During the penalty phase of her trial she confessed to joining in stabbing Mrs. La Bianca after she was dead.

With survivors of the LaBiancas sitting behind her at the California Institution for Women, Van Houten acknowledged participating in the killings ordered by Manson.

"He could never have done what he did without people like me," said Van Houten, who has been in custody for 44 years.

After years of therapy and self-examination, she said, she realizes that what she did was "like a pebble falling in a pond which affected so many people."

"I know I did something that is unforgiveable, but I can create a world where I make amends."

— Leslie Van Houten

"Mr. and Mrs. La Bianca died the worst possible deaths a human being can," she said.

Arguing to the board, Los Angeles County Deputy District Attorney Patrick Sequiera said some crimes may be an exception to the law guaranteeing the possibility of parole.

"There are certain crimes that are so heinous, so atrocious, so horrible that it should cause denial of parole," he said, elaborating on Van Houten's contradictions over the years.

In response, Van Houten's lawyer, Michael Satris, said his client "sank to the depths of Dante's inferno and she put herself there by consorting with the devil himself, Charles Manson."

Leslie Van Houten appears during her parole hearing with her attorney, Michael Satris, left, on at the California Institution for Women in Chino, Calif.

However, Satris said his client has totally reformed herself.

"Leslie committed a great sin, a great crime in 1969, and in that time (in prison) she has developed into the equal of a saint," he said. "Everything she does is for humanity."

Van Houten was portrayed at trial by her defense lawyers as the youngest and least culpable of those convicted with Manson, a young woman from a good family who had been a homecoming princess and showed promise until she became involved with drugs and was recruited into Manson's murderous cult.

Now deeply wrinkled with long gray hair tied back in a ponytail, Van Houten at times seemed near tears but did not break down at the Wednesday hearing.

She said that when she heard the Manson family had killed Tate and others, she felt left out and asked to go along the second night.

Asked if she would have done the same had children been involved, she answered, "I can't say I wouldn't have done that. I'd like to say I wouldn't, but I don't know."

Asked to explain her actions, she said, "I feel that at that point I had really lost my humanity and I can't know how far I would have gone. I had no regard for life and no measurement of my limitations."

Van Houten has previously been commended for her work helping elderly women inmates at the California Institution for Women. She earned two college degrees while in custody.

Lynette 'Squeaky' Fromme

Lynette 'Squeaky' Fromme Then

Lynette 'Squeaky' Fromme Now

For years she remained one of Manson's loyal followers, corresponding with him after many of his former followers shunned him. A spokeswoman for the prison would not say if they are still in touch.

Murder in Stockton, California

To follow through with Manson's deal with the Aryan Brotherhood, Fromme moved to Stockton, California, with Family member Nancy Pitman and a friend named Priscilla Cooper, and a pair of ex-convict Aryan Brotherhood members named Michael Monfort and James Craig. This group happened to meet up with a couple, James and Lauren Willett, at a cabin. The ex-convicts forced James Willett to dig his own grave and gunned him down because he was going to tell the authorities about a series of robberies that the ex-convicts had committed after they were released from prison. After the body of James Willett was found, with his hand still sticking out of the ground, the housemates were taken into custody on suspicion of murder. After their arrest, the body of Lauren Willett was discovered as well. An infant girl believed to be the Willetts' daughter was also found in the house in Stockton, and placed with Mary Graham Hall. Fromme was released for lack of evidence.

The Sonoma County coroner's office concluded that James Willett was killed sometime in September 1972 although his body was not found until the beginning of November 1972. He had been buried near Guerneville in Sonoma County. On the night of Saturday November 11, 1972, the Stockton Police responded to information that a station wagon owned by the Willetts was in the area. It was discovered parked in front of 720 W. Flora Street. "Police Sgt. Richard Whiteman went to the house and, when he was refused entry, forced his way in. All the persons subsequently arrested were in the house except for Miss Fromme. She telephoned the house while police were there, asking to be picked up, and officers obliged, taking her into custody nearby. Police found a quantity of guns and ammunition in the house along with amounts of marijuana, and noticed freshly dug earth beneath the building."

The Stockton Police obtained a warrant and dug up the body of Lauren Willett around 5 a.m. the following day. Cooper told investigators that Lauren had been shot accidentally and had been buried when they realized she was dead. Cooper contended that Monfort was "demonstrating the dangers of firearms, playing a form of Russian roulette with a .38 caliber pistol" and had first spun the gun cylinder and shot at his own head, and when the gun didn't fire, pointed it at the victim, whereupon it fired. The Stockton Police indicated that Lauren Willett "was with the others of her own volition prior to the shooting, and was not being held prisoner."

Fromme was held in custody for two and a half months but never charged. The other four people involved were convicted. In an interview from the San Joaquin County Jail, she told reporters that she had been traveling in California trying to visit "brothers" in jail and to visit Manson. Fromme said that she came to Stockton to visit William Goucher, who was already in jail on a robbery charge when Mrs. Willett died. She claimed to be innocent of any wrongdoing. "They told me I was being put in here for murder because I didn't have anything to say." She also said from jail, "I know there are lots of people who've spent time for being quiet. That's why Charlie is in jail."

Fromme stated that she took a bus from Los Angeles to Stockton on Friday November 10, 1972, to visit Goucher, whom she described as "a brother". She called Pitman, she said, and spent Friday night at the Flora Street house. When she left the jail after visiting Goucher Saturday, she called the house "to ask someone to pick me up". Stockton Police traced the call and arrested her at a phone booth.

After leaving Stockton, Fromme moved into a Sacramento apartment with fellow Manson family member Sandra Good. The two wore robes on occasion and changed their names to symbolize their devotion to Manson's new religion, Fromme becoming "Red" in honor of her red hair and the redwoods, and Good, "Blue", for her blue eyes and the ocean; both nicknames were originally given to them by Manson.

Attempt to contact Jimmy Page

In March 1975, during Led Zeppelin's 1975 North American concert tour, Fromme spoke with Danny Goldberg, the vice president of the band's record company at the hotel the band was staying at in L.A. She asked to meet with guitarist Jimmy Page to warn him of "bad energy." Fromme claimed to have foreseen the future and wished to forewarn Page of the imminent danger. Goldberg stated that even he couldn't see Page until the following night, to which Fromme responded "tomorrow night will probably be too late." After a long discussion, Goldberg agreed to deliver a message to Page if she were to commit it to writing. Allegedly, the note was burned.

Assassination attempt on President Ford

On the morning of September 5, 1975, Fromme went to Sacramento's Capitol Park (reportedly to plead with President Gerald Ford about the plight of the California redwoods) dressed in a nun-like red robe and armed with a Colt M1911 .45 semi-automatic pistol that she pointed at Ford. The pistol's magazine was loaded with four rounds, but there was no cartridge in the chamber. She was immediately restrained by Larry Buendorf, a Secret Service agent. While being further restrained and handcuffed, Fromme managed to say a few sentences to the on-scene cameras, emphasizing that the gun "didn't go off". Her 1975 arrest as shown by her sitting in a U.S. Marshal's vehicle as she waits to be brought to jail in 1975 is an image that continues to get frequent use. In 1980, Fromme told *The Sacramento Bee* that she had deliberately ejected the cartridge in her weapon's chamber before leaving home that morning.

After a lengthy trial in which she refused to cooperate with her own defense, she was convicted of the attempted assassination of the president and received a life sentence under a 1965 law which made attempted presidential assassinations a federal crime punishable by a maximum sentence of life in prison. When U.S. Attorney Dwayne Keyes recommended severe punishment because she was "full of hate and violence," Fromme threw an apple at him, hitting him in the face and knocking off his glasses.

"I stood up and waved a gun (at Ford) for a reason," said Fromme. "I was so relieved not to have to shoot it, but, in truth, I came to get life. Not just my life but clean air, healthy water and respect for creatures and creation."

Aftermath

Seventeen days after Fromme's arrest, Sara Jane Moore attempted to assassinate Ford outside the St. Francis Hotel in San Francisco. Moore was restrained by bystander Oliver Sipple, a decorated veteran, and the single shot fired from her gun slightly injured taxi driver John Ludwig, who was standing inside the hotel.

In 1979, Fromme was transferred out of Federal Correctional Institution, Dublin in Dublin, California, for attacking a fellow inmate, Julienne Bušić, with the claw-end of a hammer. On December 23, 1987, she escaped from the Federal Prison Camp, Alderson in Alderson, West Virginia, attempting to meet Manson, who she had heard had testicular cancer. She was captured again two days later and incarcerated at the Federal Medical Center, Carswell in Fort Worth, Texas.

The Colt M1911 .45-caliber pistol used by Fromme in her assassination attempt on Gerald Ford

Fromme first became eligible for parole in 1985, and was entitled by federal law to a mandatory hearing after 30 years, but could waive that hearing and apply for release at a later date. Fromme steadfastly waived her right to request a hearing and was required by federal law to complete a parole application before one could be considered and granted. Fromme was granted parole in July 2008, but was not released because of the extra time added to her sentence for the 1987 prison escape.

Fromme, Federal Bureau of Prisons #06075-180 was released on parole from Federal Medical Center, Carswell on August 14, 2009. She then reportedly moved to Marcy, New York.

Charles "Tex" Watson

Charles "Tex" Watson Then

Charles "Tex" Watson Now

Charles "Tex" Watson is also serving a life sentence for the Tate/LaBianca murders, and is currently housed in Mule Creek State Prison in Northern California.

During his time in prison, Watson has converted to Christianity, written several books, married, fathered four children and trained as a minister of religion. His wife, Kristin and their family live close to the prison where she operates a Web site for their ministry called *Abounding Love Ministries, Inc.*

On October 10, 2001, Watson was turned down again for parole at his thirteenth parole hearing and was told not to apply for another four years.

The Associated Press stated, "Watson made a personal appeal to the two-member panel of the California Board of Prison Terms, saying he takes full responsibility for his crimes and is now a different person who would never do such things again." However, a prison correctional counselor said that "Watson still poses an unpredictable threat to the community should he be released."

Debra Tate, the sister of the brutally murdered Sharon Tate Polanski, tearfully urged the board to deny Watson's request.

His last hearing was in November 2011. He received a five-year denial, rather than a 7-10-15 year maximum.

His next scheduled parole hearing is in November 2016.

Susan "Sadie" Denise Atkins

Susan "Sadie" Denise Atkins Then

Susan "Sadie" Denise Atkins Prison photo

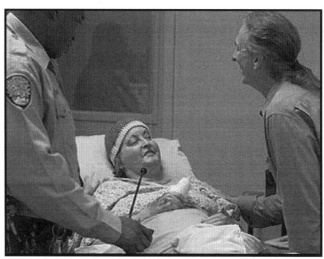
In her last days

Susan "Sadie" Denise Atkins served her life sentence at California Institution for Women at Frontera. During her time in prison Atkins married twice.

In September 2009, at age 61, suffering from terminal brain cancer, Susan Adkins faced her 13th parole hearing. According to a website maintained by her husband and attorney James Whitehouse, with 85 percent of her body paralyzed she could no longer sit up or be moved to a wheelchair. Even so, Whitehouse knew there was still a chance that the parole board would find her release to be a danger to society. Adkins was known among members of the Manson Family as Sadie Mae Glutz, and by her own admission held pregnant actress Sharon Tate down and killed her, stabbing her 16 times. At a parole hearing in 1993 she said that Tate had "asked me to let her baby live....I told her I didn't have any mercy on her."

Vincent Bugliosi, who prosecuted Atkins, said he was not opposed to her release given her current condition, adding that she had paid "substantially, though not completely, for her horrendous crimes. Paying completely would mean imposing the death penalty." Bugliosi also stated that he supported her release in order to save the state money. The cost for Atkins' medical care since she was hospitalized on March 18, 2008, "has reportedly surpassed $1.15 million with additional cost of over $300,000 to guard her hospital room." Bugliosi stated that he was challenging the notion that "just because Susan Atkins showed no mercy to her victims, we therefore are duty-bound to follow her inhumanity and show no mercy to her." Former prosecutor Stephen R. Kay, who also prosecuted Manson supporters, opposed Atkins' release, stating:

Kay also stated that he had attended about 60 parole hearings related to the murders and spent considerable time with the victims' families, witnessing their suffering.

Los Angeles County District Attorney Steve Cooley stated that he was strongly opposed to the release, saying in a letter to the board it would be "an affront to people of this state, the California criminal justice system and the next of kin of many murder victims."

Cooley wrote that Atkins' "horrific crimes alone warrant a denial of her request" and that she "failed to demonstrate genuine remorse and lacks insight and understanding of the gravity of her crimes." Suzan Hubbard, director of adult prisons in California, also recommended against granting Atkins' request. California Governor Arnold Schwarzenegger also opposed Atkins' release, stating that: "I don't believe in compassionate release. I think that they have to stay in, they have to serve their time ... Those kinds of crimes are just so unbelievable that I'm not for the compassionate release."

Orange County District Attorney Tony Rackauckas also opposed Atkins' release, stating that "It would be a grave miscarriage of justice to burden the citizens of Orange County by paroling her to Orange County, where she can enjoy the comforts of her husband, home and mercy she did not show Sharon Tate [or] her unborn baby."

Atkins' release hearing took place on July 15, 2008. During the 90-minute hearing, emotional pleas were made by both supporters and opponents of Atkins' release. The public hearing limited speakers' comments to five minutes each. After the board heard the case (as well as other agenda items), it retired to closed session for final deliberations. Due to her failing health, Atkins herself did not attend the hearing.

Debra Tate, the only surviving immediate relative of murder victim Sharon Tate, spoke in opposition to a compassionate release for Atkins, stating, "She will be set free when judged by God. It's important that she die in incarceration." Pam Turner, a cousin of Sharon Tate, also opposed Atkins' release, stating, "If she were capable of comprehending what our family's been through, she would be ashamed to come before this parole board and ask such a request." Anthony DiMaria, the nephew of murder victim Thomas Jay Sebring, also opposed Atkins' release, stating, "You will hear various opinions with respect to this today, but you will hear nothing from the nine people who lie in their graves and suffered horrendous deaths at the hands of Susan Atkins."

Gloria Goodwin Killian, director of ACWIP (Action Committee for Women in Prison) and a Pasadena legal researcher and prisoner advocate, spoke in support for Atkins' compassionate release, arguing, "Susan has been punished all that she can be. Short of going out to the hospital and physically torturing her, there is nothing left anyone can do to her. The people who are suffering are the people you see in this room today." In July 2008, Atkins' husband, James W. Whitehouse, told the board, "They tell me we're lucky if we have three months. It's not going to be fun. It's not going to be pretty."

The 11 members of the California Board of Parole Hearings ultimately denied Atkins' request in a unanimous decision after final deliberations. The decision — posted on its Web site — meant the Atkins' request would not be forwarded to the Los Angeles Superior Court that sentenced her, which would have had the final say as to whether or not she would be released. On September 24, 2008, Atkins was transferred back to the Central California Women's Facility in Chowchilla, California to the facility's skilled nursing center.

Prior to her 2009 parole hearing, a website maintained by Atkins' husband claimed that she was paralyzed over 85 percent of her body and unable to sit up or be transferred to a wheelchair.

For the eighteenth and final time, Atkins was denied parole on September 2, 2009. On September 3, the parole board denied her release. She would have been able to try again in 2012, but died on Thursday September 24, 2009, at the Central California Women's facility in Chowchilla. A prison spokesman announced to reporters that her cause of death was listed as natural causes because her family did not request an autopsy. Her husband, James Whitehouse, subsequently released the following statement: "Susan passed away peacefully surrounded by friends and loved ones and the incredible staff at the Skilled Nursing Facility at the Central California Women's Facility ... Her last whispered word was 'Amen.' "

On September 3, the parole board denied her release. She would have been able to try again in 2012, but died on Thursday September 24, 2009.

Patricia "Katie" Krenwinkel

Patricia "Katie" Krenwinkel Then

Patricia "Katie" Krenwinkel Now

Krenwinkel, still incarcerated, is now at the California Institution for Women in Chino, California. In an interview conducted by Diane Sawyer in 1994, Krenwinkel stated: "I wake up every day knowing that I'm a destroyer of the most precious thing, which is life; and I do that because that's what I deserve, is to wake up every morning and know that." During that same interview, Patricia expressed the most remorse for what she did to Folger, telling Diane Sawyer, "That was just a young woman that I killed, who had parents. She was supposed to live a life and her parents were never supposed to see her dead."

During a 2004 parole hearing, when asked who she would place at the top of the list of people she has harmed, Patricia Krenwinkel responded, "Myself." She was denied parole following that hearing because, according to the panel, Krenwinkel still posed an "unacceptable risk to public safety". In total, Krenwinkel has been denied parole thirteen times; her last hearing was in January 2011. The two-member parole board said after the hearing in Los Angeles that the 63-year-old Krenwinkel would not be eligible for parole again for seven years. The panel said they were swayed by the memory of the crimes, along with 80 letters which came from all over the world urging Patricia Krenwinkel's continued incarceration.

Krenwinkel, is the longest-serving female prisoner in the California prison system — a distinction she gained when fellow Charles Manson follower Susan Atkins died in 2009.

Linda Kasabian

Linda Kasabian Then

Linda Kasabian Now

Linda Kasabian was granted immunity for giving evidence against Manson and other family members. Following the trial she left California.

 The heavy news media coverage of the Manson trial had made Linda Kasabian a well-known, if somewhat controversial, figure by the time the sentences had been handed down, with opinions about her ranging from sympathetic to hostile. Kasabian shortly returned to New Hampshire with her husband and her children, seeking to escape the glare of the media, and to raise her children quietly. She lived on a hippie commune for a time and worked as a cook later.

Kasabian was called back to Los Angeles County several times after the first trial: she was a witness against Tex Watson in his separate trial in 1971, and also against Leslie Van Houten in her two retrials in 1977. Linda Kasabian later divorced her husband Robert Kasabian, and eventually she remarried.

Kasabian was detained for numerous traffic violations, until an automobile accident left her partially disabled. During an Easter celebration in New Hampshire in 1978, she and some friends interfered with firemen who were attempting to extinguish a bonfire. Though she had severed all of her ties with the Manson "family", the Secret Service kept her under surveillance for a time after her former Manson associate Lynette "Squeaky" Fromme attempted to assassinate President Gerald Ford. Kasabian was the target of scorn from the few remaining Manson "family" members.

Over the years, Kasabian has avoided and refused most news media attention. She appeared only once from 1969 to 2008, for an interview with the syndicated American television program *A Current Affair* in 1988.

Most recently, Cineflix, a production company in the United Kingdom and Canada, produced a docu-drama called *Manson*, in which Kasabian appears, telling her story in complete detail for the first time. This program was telecast in the UK on August 10, 2009, and also in the United States on Sept. 7, 2009 and again on July 20, 2013, on the History Channel. In this taped interview, Kasabian recounts her four weeks spent with the Manson "family". Her image is slightly obscured to protect her identity.

In a September 2, 2009 live interview on CNN's *Larry King Live*, Kasabian recounted her memories of the murders at Sharon Tate's home. To help her maintain her now-quiet life, Kasabian wore a disguise provided by the program during her interview. She told King during the interview that after the trial she had been in need of, but had never obtained, "psychological counseling", and that during the previous 12 years, she had been "on a path of healing and rehabilitation." When asked about the degree of remorse she felt for her participation in the crimes, Kasabian said that she felt as though she took on all the guilt that "no one else who was involved in the crimes felt guilt for", apparently referring to the fact that, even during her own court testimony, the co-defendants in the case showed extreme nonchalance when faced with such gruesome murders.

Sandra Good

Sandra Good Then

Sandra Good Now

On December 22, 1975, Good and another Manson devotee, Susan Murphy, were indicted for "conspiracy to send threatening letters through the mail" by a Federal Grand Jury in Sacramento, in connection with death threats against more than 170 corporate executives who Good believed (see ATWA) were polluting the earth.

Found guilty on March 16, 1976, Good was sentenced on April 13, to 15 years in prison.

Good was paroled in early December 1985, after having served nearly 10 years. Unlike many of the Family members, Good still professed total allegiance to Manson.

A stipulation of her parole was that she could not return to California. She moved to Vermont, where she lived quietly under the name Sandra Collins until 1989, when her environmental activism made the news and her identity was made public.

After her time on parole ended, Good moved to Hanford, California, near Corcoran State Prison, to be closer to Manson, although she was not allowed to visit him. On January 26, 1996, she and George Stimson began a pro-Manson website, on which they claimed to have the true source of Manson thought. She also supported Manson's environmental movement, ATWA (Air Trees Water Animals). The website went offline in 2001, but in 2011 Good's website was relaunched.

Sandra Good has since left Hanford, and she and Stimson have made no public statements in support of Manson.

Steve "Clem" Grogan

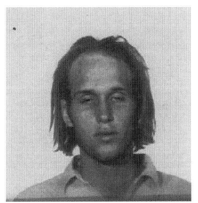

Steve "Clem" Grogan Then

Steve "Clem" Grogan Now

Grogan later helped Manson, Watson and Bruce Davis to kill Spahn ranch hand Donald "Shorty" Shea. The jury returned verdicts of life imprisonment for Manson and Davis, but death for Grogan. However, on December 23, 1971, Judge James Kolts stated that "Grogan was too stupid and too hopped on drugs to decide anything on his own" and that it was really Manson "who decided who lived or died" and reduced Grogan's sentence to life imprisonment. Grogan later assisted the authorities and drew a map to where Shea's body was buried. In prison he was head of the prison's program to deter juveniles from a life of crime and kept away from fellow inmate Manson. Grogan also played guitar and sang in the Freedom Orchestra Band with fellow Manson family co-conspirator Bobby Beausoleil when they both served time at the Deuel Vocational Institute in Tracy, California. Beausoleil later revealed that he convinced Grogan to begin playing again and even made him a guitar. He was released from prison in 1985 and remains the only Manson family member who has been convicted of murder and released from prison.

Bruce Davis

Bruce Davis Then

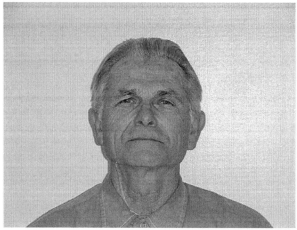

Bruce Davis Now

Bruce Davis is serving a life sentence in the California Men's Colony, San Luis Obispo, for the murders of Gary Hinman and Donald Shea. He attended his twenty seventh parole hearing in March of 2013.   Parole was again refused.

Mr. Davis would have been only the second Manson-related murder convict to be granted parole since the killings began in 1969.

Bobby Beausoleil

Bobby Beausoleil Then

Bobby Beausoleil Now

Convicted in 1969 for his part in the murder of Gary Hinman, he remains in prison despite numerous appeals and bail applications. He married in 1982 and is currently serving out his time in Oregon after being transferred there in 1993 at his own request.

It seems, Bobby Beausoleil was something of an entrepreneur back in 1984. He was apparently running a business out of his prison cell called "B & B Enterprises." The company consisted of himself, of course, and his wife, according to prison officials. An actual lieutenant from the prison security team at CMC wrote Beausoleil up, and filled out a report, which is summarized here:

"Approximately mid-December of 1984 Inmate Beausoleil received in the institution mail a large manila envelope containing Xerox copies of the following. Number one, letters of correspondence with people from various states. These letters pertained to purchase orders of child pornography, ages between four and 12 years old. The types of orders were photographs, movies, tape cassettes and magazines. They were all specific as to what they preferred, age, sex and nationality. Two, photocopies of order forms with names and addresses of purchasers with their money order or check made out to B&B Enterprise. A few money orders were made out to R. Beausoleil in care of B&B Enterprises. Three, one letter pertained to a person offering his services to B&B Enterprise by making movies or magazines for him, meaning Beausoleil. In this letter the man stated that he and an accomplice kidnapped children between the ages of four and eight years old. They moved from one state to another every three months to stay ahead of the law. Some states he mentioned were Florida, Washington DC, Colorado, and the last state in which they had just left was Arizona. He mentioned after their stay in California they were heading to Washington. Four, photocopies of bank records showing deposits to B&B Enterprise and R. Beausoleil. All of this information came with a return address of B&B Enterprise, P.O. Box 1033 in Grover City." Which I believe is where Mr. Beausoleil's wife was living at the time. *"In the second week of February, Inmate Beausoleil received another manila envelope from B&B Enterprise in Grover City. This envelope contained purchase orders for magazines containing -- which contained nothing but child spanking and beatings. Each one asked for a certain age, sex and nationality. The order forms were addressed to Sassy Bottoms, B&B Enterprises, P.O. Box 1033, Grover City, California 93433."*

He has spent his 30-plus years in prison focused on electronic music and video production. He has also cultivated a number of sponsors, which has resulted in the creation of a video production and audio recording studio in the prison. He is now the director of the Los Hermanos video project and has made 9 videos for "at risk" children. He has also made videos that help prisoners develop cognitive skills that will hopefully reduce recidivism.

10050 Cielo Drive

10050 Cielo Drive in 1969

10050 Cielo Drive (now 10066 **Cielo Drive**), as it looks today

The Crime Scene

According to an August 1999 *Reuters* news service report the house at 10050 Cielo Drive, rented by Roman Polanski and Sharon Tate at the time of the murders, was demolished in 1994.   An Italian- style mansion has been erected in its place and the street address has been changed. The new mansion was originally priced at $12.5 million in an attempt to cash in on the locations notoriety but no sale was made.   Recently, the price was reduced to $7.7 million but the house still remains vacant.

3301 Waverly Drive

3301 Waverly Drive Then

3301 Waverly Drive now
The address was changed to 3311 Waverly drive and a second driveway and a gate has since been added to the property.

Spahn Ranch

Spahn Ranch in 1969

Spahn Ranch as it looks today

The original headquarters of the Manson family is also on the market. The 43-acre property at Chatsworth, minus the ranch house, which burnt down some time ago, is selling for $2.7 million.

In Closing

No other crime in history had such an impact as the Manson murders in the late 60's. Today some people feel that Charles Manson should not have been given such a harsh punishment as he was not present at the crime scene. Others feel that the followers that where released from prison got off way too easy.

Look for these and other great books By David Pietras

From "Mommy to Monster"

The "Daddy Dearest" Club

The Manson Family "Then and Now"

When Love Kills

The Making of a Nightmare

THE INFAMOUS "FLORIDA 5"

Death, Murder, and Vampires Real Vampire Stories

The Life and Death of Richard Ramirez, The Night Stalker (History's Killers Unmasked Series)

Profiling The Killer of a Childhood Beauty Queen

No Justice For Caylee Anthony

A Texas Style Witch Hunt "Justice Denied" The Darlie Lynn Routier Story by

The Book of Revelations Explained The End Times

Murder of a Childhood

John Gotti: A True Mafia Don (History's Killers Unmasked Series)

MURDERED FOR HIS MILLIONS The Abraham Shakespeare Case

The Son of Sam "Then and Now" The David Berkowitz Story

A LOOK INSIDE THE FIVE MAFIA FAMILIES OF NEW YORK CITY

Unmasking The Real Hannibal Lecter

Top 10 Most Haunted Places in America

40 minutes in Abbottabad The Raid on Osama bin Laden

In The Footsteps of a Hero The Military Journey of General David H. Petraeus

BATTLEFIELD BENGHAZI

CASE CLOSED The State of Florida vs. George Zimmerman THE TRUTH REVEALED

CROSSING THE THIN BLUE LINE

THE GHOST FROM MY CHILDHOOD A TRUE GHOST STORY ABOUT THE GELSTON CASTLE AND THE GHOST OF "AUNT" HARRIET DOUGLAS...

Haunted United Kingdom

In Search of Jack the Ripper (History's Killers Unmasked Series)

The Last Ride of Bonnie and Clyde

The Meaning of a Tragedy Canada's Serial Killers Revealed

MOMSTER

Murder In The Kingdom

The Shroud of Turin and the Mystery Surrounding Its Authenticity

The Unexplained World That We Live In

Made in the USA
Middletown, DE
12 January 2016